'OGGIE' TELLAM'S
SECOND
BOOK OF CORNISH LIMERICKS

DAVID 'OGGIE' TELLAM

Rose, Aug '10
To Remind you of
your stay in Cornwall,
love Sam x.

Acknowledgements

There are many people who have encouraged me to compose another book of Cornish Limericks. To all of whom I tender my sincere thanks.
To the following I owe special thanks; Brian Tellam for his enhancement of the cartoon drawings – Jean Tellam for her help with proof reading, but I am most indebted to Clive Baker who carried out the computer work, assisted with the proof reading and being a student and also a teacher of the Cornish language was able to establish the place names of the chosen locations in the Cornish language, with the aid and research of Craig Weatherhill's book, "Place Names in Cornwall and Scilly", a "Westcountry Guide" by Wessex Books.

All rights reserved. No part of this publication may be reproduced, converted or archived into any other medium without a relevant permission first being obtained from the publisher. Nor should the book be circulated or resold in any binding other than its original cover.

Oggie Tellam's Second Book of Cornish Limericks

© David 'Oggie' Tellam

First edition published 2007

Published by:
Palores Publications
Redruth, Kernow

Printed by:
The Print Consultancy
21, Timber St., Chippenham, Wilts., SN15 3BS

ISBN 978-0-9556682-2-7

INTRODUCTION

I WAS once told by an aunt that I showed a very early disposition to rhyming speech.

She informed me that at the time when I was being weaned from the milk bottle, an elder brother, in the absence of my parents, filled an empty bottle with Guinness. He was himself too young to be prosecuted for supplying alcohol to a minor—but he was duly chastised by our father when he discovered that a bottle of Guinness had gone missing from the crate, which he kept under his bed.

It was too late, the damage had been done.

Apparently, when the next feeding time came around, I was said to scream:

"Dada, Mama, kiss-kiss, kiss-kiss!
Dada, Mama, Gin-giss, Gin-giss!"

Thus began the original words of my limerick form.

* * * * * *

AUTHOR'S NOTES

On each of the photographs will be seen some words in Cornish. The first word(s) show the earliest known form of the place name, whilst those in brackets represent the actual spelling in unified Cornish, based on the middle Cornish period.

E.g Vellyn trukkya (melyn drokkya) ... for "Valley Truckle"

There are some abbreviations used:
OE = Old English
OC = Old Cornish
LC = Late Cornish
Fr = French

For more information regarding the place names, please refer to Craig Weatherhill's book, "Place Names in Cornwall and Scilly" published by Wessex Books.

DEDICATION

Dedicated to Councillor Roy Lobb

A LEADING light who served the Parish of Chacewater for some thirty years, and the District of Carrick for a quarter of a century.

Of the many achievements of this nonagenarian, he was instrumental in; the establishment of Chacewater Health Centre, the Bowling Club, and the advanced status of Chacewater A.F.C.

He gave his all but took nothing.

Ny wra-ef vodya an bys-ma,
Den bras y golon hep gormola.

Port Wrickel (porth wykkel)

A vegan who lived in Portwrinkle,
On salads, fresh spices would sprinkle,
With celery salt,
And vinegar malt;
Tantalising, tickled taste buds, to tinkle.

Beaurepere (beau repair, Fr)

A long legged man from Barripper,
Slipped onto his foot a new slipper.
But unlucky for him,
He then slipped on a skin.
After having just slipped on a slipper.

Trewarvene (tre war venedh)

A tortoise that lived in Tintagel,
Whose movements were not at all agile,
Won his fame; fair and square,
In a race with a hare.
But the process was painfully gradual.

Geevor mine near St Just   Lanuste (lan Ust)

A young miner who lived in St Just,
Though physically strong and robust,
Met a problem while thinking,
Of a shaft, needing sinking;
He'll soon get to its bottom, we trust.

Rosevinney (ros fynny)
(LC ros fydny)

A sour young man from Rosevidney,
Who developed a stone in his kidney,
Became a lot sweeter,
When it cleared his ureter.
But he had a tough time of it - didn' e?

Gwynyar (after St Guinier)

A very tall lady from Gwinear,
With a bearing decidedly linear,
Lived for ninety nine days,
On cold mayonnaise.
Now she's also decidedly skinnier.

A farmers wife from Trerice,
Cut the tails off three blind mice.
To renew them, they wrote,
To a bloke, for a quote.
And he bettered the retailing price.

A young Mountain Goat from St Veep,
Who found a high peak far to steep,
Had studied new tactics,
So improved his gymnastics.
To advance by a mighty big leap.

S. Vep (after St. Vepe)

Amaleglos (amal eglos)

Rambling barefoot around Chapel Amble,
A hiker who'd trod on a bramble,
Had, for the first half a mile,
Shown impeccable style.
A preamble to a ramble cum shamble.

Heyl (heyl)

A wandering family from Hayle,
Who wandered up hill and down dale,
Kept changing abodes,
As they took to the roads.
Seemed to name all their houses 'For Sale'.

A careless Young man from St Issey.
Who crashed in his dad's old 'Tin Lizzie',
Cried out, shedding tears,
"I will pay for repairs!"
So he's not such a bad fellow, is he?

S. Ydi (after St. Idi)

Lansteventon (lan Stefan)

The people who live up in Lans' on.
Run awry when they go out a danc' in.
They skip round the town.
Up the hills and then down.
With their thoughts fully set on romanc' in.

Marghasyou (marghas Yow)
(or)Marghasbian (marghas vyghan)

Said a bather from Mar-a-zi-on,
Who had lain on a spot she might dry on,
"Now the tide's getting high,
And I'm not at all dry.
Is there no place that one can re-lie on?"

Cripples ease (from English)

When soaring above Cripplesease,
A glider crashed down on some trees.
But a report in his journal,
Claimed a tepid shy thermal,
Became stuck on a weak fickle breeze.

Coysgaran (cos garan)

There was a young maid from Cusgarne,
Who tripped on a bale in the barn.
There was nothing more shocking,
Than a tear in her stocking.
She said, "darn it!" and did with some yarn.

Fraddam (forth +??)

Fair Eve, a young Lady from Fraddam,
In the garden took an apple from Adam.
Now, was Eve so naive,
As two sons to conceive;
Or, was she a knowing young madam?

Five Lanes (from English)

An inventor who lived in Five Lanes,
Was always working his brains,
On dreaming up schemes.
But a load of pipe dreams,
Was all that he got for his pains.

Egloshallow (eglos hallow) (or) after St Ylocan

There was an old man from Illogan,
Who planted potatoes and dug 'em.
He started with four.
Now he's got many more.
All he needs now is someone to scrub 'em.

A daring young maiden from Newquay,
Bodged a plane from her dad's old Suzuki.
Now they say she's insane,
Up and round in her plane,
But she claims that she's just going loopy.

Penhallow (pen hallow)

On traffic patrol in Penhallow,
A warden said, "Hey my good fellow!
You've crossed a red light,
With a green; that's not right!
Now we've only got amber and yellow".

Named after The Levant

A young fellow who lives in Levant.
On wooing Miss Trewin is bent.
But the lovely Miss Trewin,
Has other plans brew'in.
She's persu'in a gent more gallant.

Penzance (pen sans)

Some pirates approaching Penzance,
Sent out several spies in advance.
But had a surprise,
When they heard local cries,
"Come ashore it is only ten pence!"

Lostuiudiel (lost wedhyel)

A grumpy old man from Lostwithiel,
Whose complaints were always so trivial,
Was given some potions,
To calm his emotions,
Now, old 'Grumpy' is much more convivial.

Cayn, Seynt Keyn, (after female St Kayn)

Said a 'Rain Maker' who lived in St Keyne,
"The Well has gone dry; what a shame!"
So he chanted a spell,
To replenish the Well.
With the spell, the Well's well, once again.

Marassanvose (marghas an vos)

A somnambulist from Marazanvose,
While in a deep state of repose,
Trekked the Moon and the stars,
Paid a visit to Mars,
Then crept back to his bed on tip toes.

A Clairvoyant who lived in Callestick,
Had set himself up as a mystic.
For ten pounds he would claim;
To bring fortune and fame,
But he's yet to see someone who'd risk it.

Said a milkman who worked in Penzance,
"For the theft of my milk, I'm incensed.
I've no inkling of doubt,
There's a 'Humphrey' about,
And he's sold all my milk through a 'fence'!"

Castelboterel (castel Boterel)

Identical twins in Boscastle,
Had their names embossed on a tassel,
Which were hung round their necks,
So as not to perplex;
Thus avoiding confusion and hassle.

Godrevy (godrevy)

A Cornishman adrift at Godrevy,
Lost power when his engine went queasy.
So he set up a sail,
And beat tracks into Hayle.
Just as well that the weather was breezy!

Heyl (heyl)

Eglosmeylyon (eglos Melan)

A dissenting young rebel from Mullion,
Who worked aboard ship as a scullion,
Knew his P's and his Q's,
But confused E's with U's
And stirred up a bad spell of rubullion?

From a spire on a church up in Truro,
Said a Weather Vane, taunting a Sparrow,
"Indeed I'm not vain!
It's quite plain I'm a vane.
So! Bear my vein of disdain till tomorrow!"

after St Maudet
Lanvausa (lan Vausa)

A naive young hen at St Mawes,
In her hen house while scratching the straws,
Found 'clay eggs' in a batch,
That she's hoping to hatch.
But she sits there just 'clutching at straws'.

Bedruthan steps (steps at bod Rudhyn)

An extremely old man from Bedruthan,
Who originally was a Redruthian,
Rammed his three-masted Barque
Into old Noah's Ark.
Was such action, then, Anti-Diluvian?

Lesard (lesard Fr.?)

A sea fearing man Timid Tizzard,
Who fell foul of a raging snow blizzard,
Came under such stress,
That he sent a distress.
"SOS, I'm in a mess off The Lizard."

38

Praze an Beeble (pras an hybel)

A falconer from Praze-An-Beeble,
Tried to hawk a reluctant young eagle.
So he gave it a shove,
To the air, from his glove,
But the effort was lazy-an' - feeble.

Trewynt (OC tre wynt)

A hunter who lived in Trewint,
Having followed the strangest foot print,
At the end of its trail,
Found a bow legged Quail,
With a leg that was strapped in a splint.

Sands at Polwragh (pol wragh)

With its head buried deep in Praa Sands,
An Ostrich had made several stands.
But the best of its plumage,
Sustained severe damage,
Ending up in two ladies' hat bands.

Penlegh (pen legh)

A sailor who sailed from Penlee,
Met a mermaid when way out at sea.
He asked her ashore,
And they both made a tour.
Of the sea shore surrounding Penlee.

Bodrygy (bod Rygy?)

A thin teacher who taught at Bodriggy,
And known to her class as Miss Twiggy,
Did 'Maths' with aplomb,
Was 'brill' at 'Geom',
And excelled solving problems with 'Triggy'.

Cambron (cam-bron)

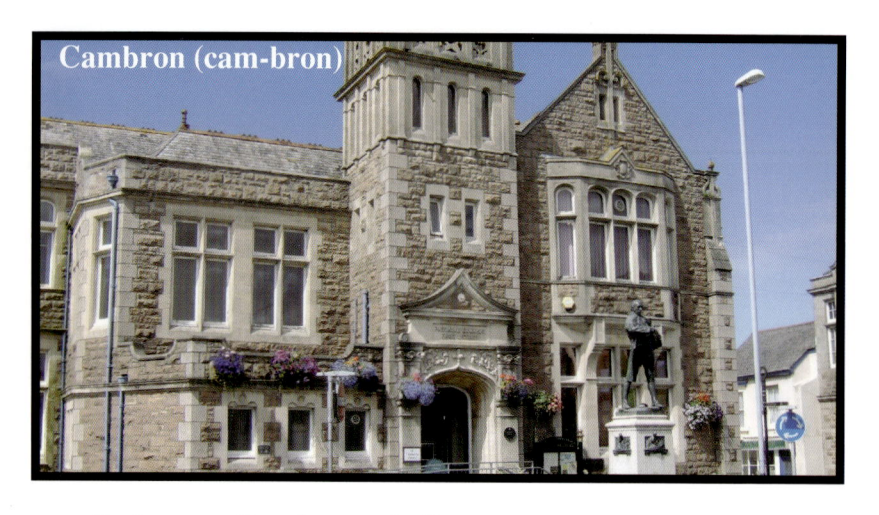

Going up Camborne hill coming down.
Going up Camborne hill coming down.
The horses stood still.
She steamed up the hill.
Going up Camborne hill coming down.

Fentongempes (fenton gempes)

*At a circus in Ventongimps,
For ten pennies you'd get a good glimpse,
Of fierce lions and tigers,
And horses and riders,
Plus a show of 'Tea partying' chimps.*

Trem (trum)

There was a young lady from Drym,
Who tried her best to keep trim.
She lived on a diet,
Of lettuce and carrot,
Which kept her all pretty and prim.

Rynsi (ryn-jy)

There was an old fellow from Rinsey,
Who had an attack of the quinsy.
So they gave him some quinine,
In a glass full to brimming.
Now he's feeling a little less flimsy.

Eglos-sans (eglos Sancres)

A gallant young knight from Sancreed,
One day rode out on his steed.
He'd heard that a dragon,
Had gone mad in Madron.
Then went forth and dispatched it with speed.

Eglosmadern (eglos Madern)

S. Cywa after St Kywa
Or Landoucho (lan Doho)

Under the shade of a tree at St Kew,
Where I asked a smart dame who I knew,
"Is that tree a Plane?"
She replied with disdain,
"To me, it's quite plain, it's a Yew!"

From the mine's bell

A Ding Dong miner fell down the Ore pass,
And feared he could smell deadly gas.
But alone in the dark,
Blamed a raspberry tart,
And some unpleasant mess he'd just passed.

Egloscury (eglos Cury)

An apprentice wine brewer from Cury,
Had brewed a new wine from his puree.
And, while judging its quality,
Raised raucous frivolity,
The verdict's still out with the jury.

Grandpont (Fr) or Ponsmur (pons mur)

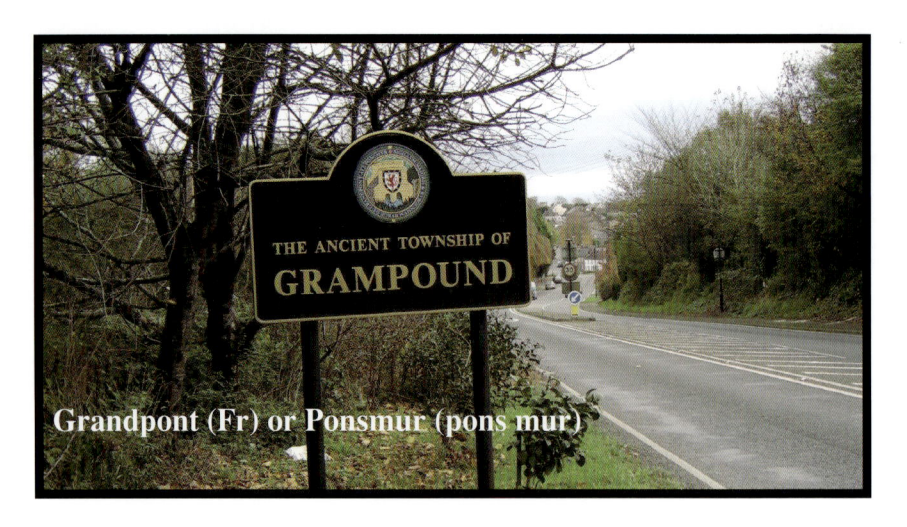

*Said a soothsayer who lived in Grampound,
"By keeping your ear to the ground,
And your nose to the grindstone.
You will head to good fortune,
And with hands full of money abound".*

Arwenack (ar Wennek)

A Falcon in flight off Falmouth,
Had harassed a young Cornish Chough,
But its mother close by,
Socked it right in the eye.
A good 'duff' from a tough Cornish Chough.

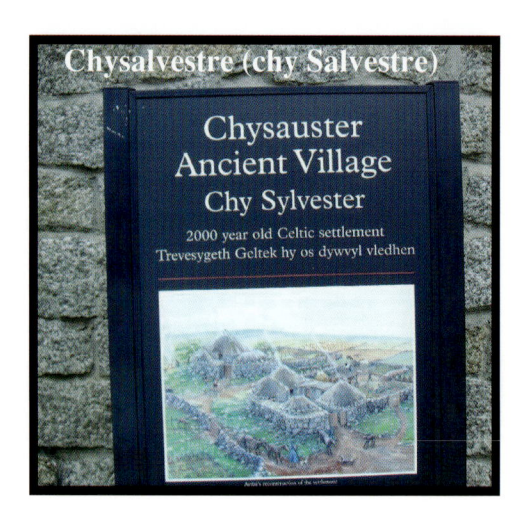

A novice at prayer in Chysauster,
Reflecting on what it might cost her,
For those flippant misdeeds,
That she truly concedes.
Now recants on her bead paternoster.

Egloskery (eglos Kery)

Now Terry from Egloskerry,
Drove to work in a bit of a hurry.
He'd used too much bottle,
When applying the throttle.
Now he's late and is ready to bury.

Lys Cerruyt (lys Kerwys)

A Card in a bar in Liskeard,
Drank his ale from a glass by the yard.
One day after lunch,
He got drunk drinking punch.
Now he's a card duly barred in Liskeard.

S. Welvela after St. Goulvel

A donkey that lived down in Gulval,
Had a head a little bit oval.
They reshaped it with clay,
Then removed it next day.
Now he's looking a little less doleful.

Pengegon (pen gygen)

A man from Pengegon called Stone,
Had an emergency call on the phone.
There was some confusion,
About a transfusion.
Did they try to get blood from a stone?

Egloslagek (eglos Lajek)

A gamekeeper who lived in Ladock,
Passed off his mistakes as bad luck.
But while herding wild deer,
Became stricken with fear,
Now he's frightened of 'passing the Buck'.

Dephryon (devryon)

There was a young lady from Dev'ran,
Who had a keen eye for the weatherman.
So she played her charts right,
And the outlook turned bright.
Now they're together, forever, well weatherin'.

Velyn-trukky (melyn drokkya)

*Moving granite down the road to Valley Truckle,
The weight had caused the wagon wheels to buckle.
Then the tyres burst their sides,
So they dragged the stone on slides.
Now they've a rut, but have no truck in Valley Truckle.*

S. Uvele (after St. Uvel)

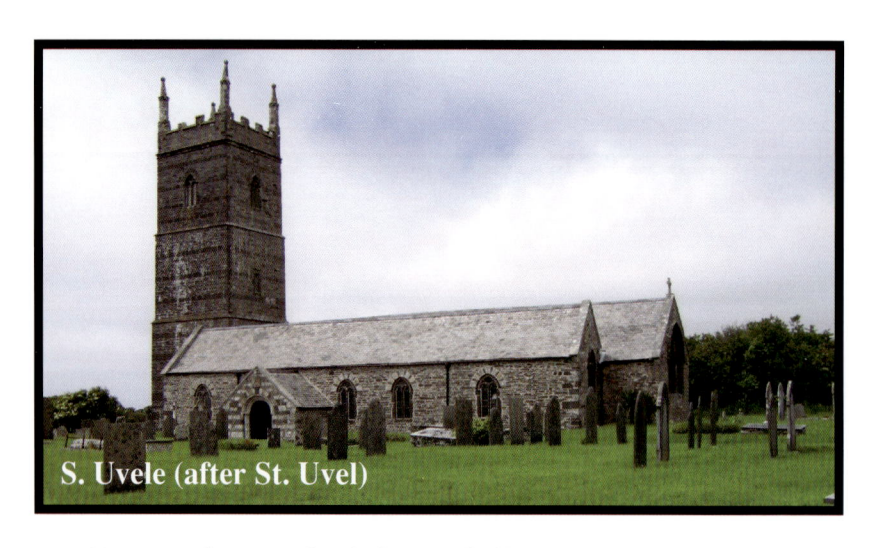

Descending a thick foggy hill at St Eval,
An apprentice was told by his devil,
"Though we've cheated and lied,
When we take one more stride,
We'll appear to be 'straight on the level' ".

Henliston (hen lys +OE tun)

On a visit we paid to Helston,
we encountered a great deal of fun.
All the good folk were merry,
As they danced in the 'Furry'.
We'll return to enjoy the next one.

Wynwala (after St. Winwalo)

All the rage on the stage in Gunwalloe,
Danced a girl who could twirl like a swallow.
Now the audience all cheered,
When her leading man appeared.
In Gunwalloe they're the hardest act to follow.

Bude (poss early celtic 'budr')

*As a conceited smart Alec from Bude,
Sunbathed in the park nearly nude,
Said two ladies when passing,
"He needs a good thrashing,
For such lewdness that lacks pulchritude".*

Egloscubert (eglos Cubert)
or Lanowyn (lan Oweyn)

At a concert, a Quintet in Cubert,
Where the players had dressed up as Rupert,
Said a critic in doubt,
"This may well be 'The Trout',
But such antics were unknown to Schubert!"

BOXHEATER
Bodmin A30

Poss from bos Zelah

Perranporth B3285

A cold hearted man from Boxheater,
Addicted to Chile saltpetre,
Found this habit was halted,
When he got fully salted.
Now his heart's turning warm and lots sweeter.

Restormel (ros tor-mol)

There's a diurnal ghost at Restormel,
Whose habits are strangely informal.
In his flowing black shrouds,
He attracts massive crowds.
For a ghost, he's most surely abnormal!

68